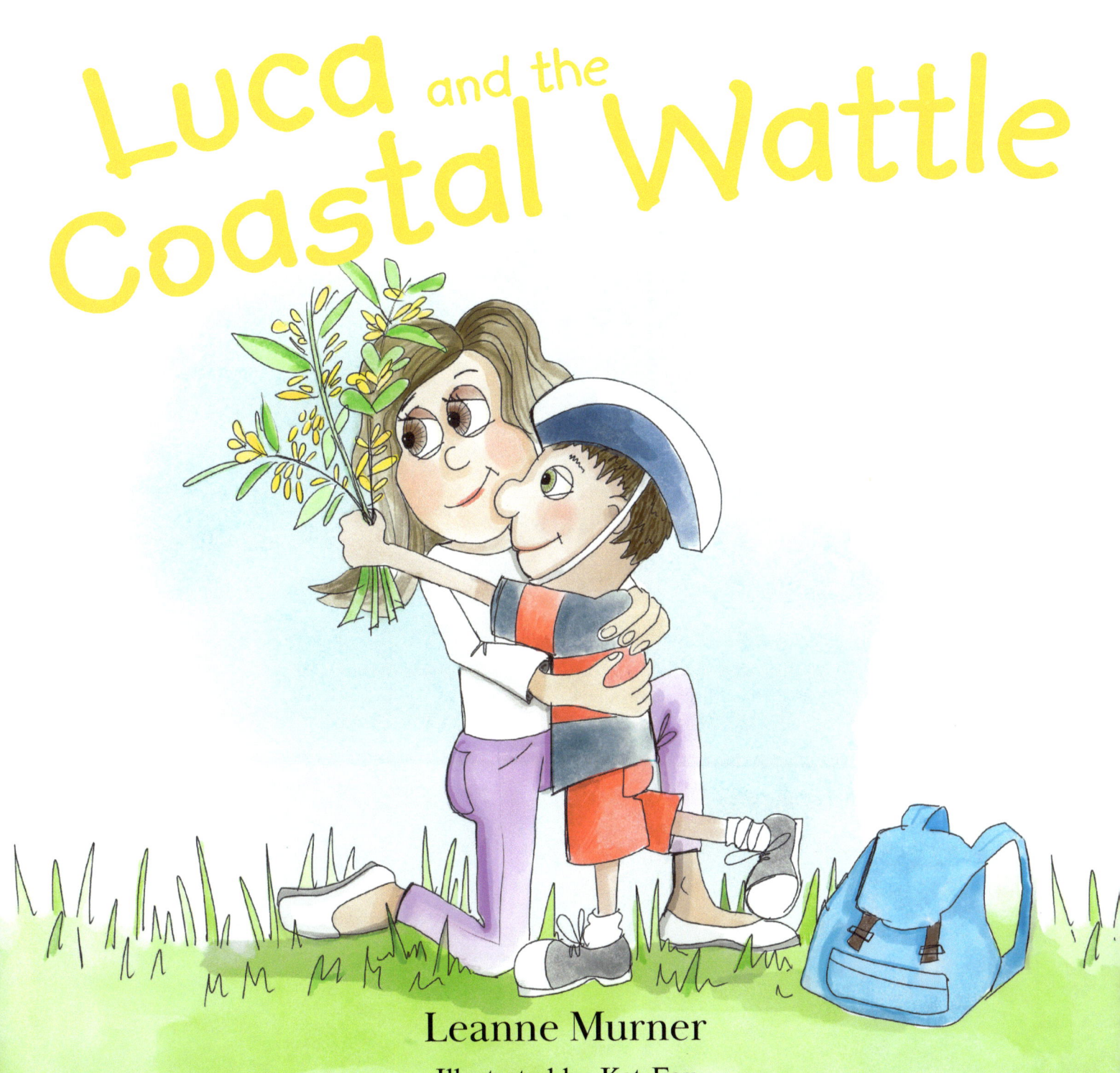

# Luca and the Coastal Wattle

Leanne Murner

Illustrated by Kat Fox

Serenity Press Pty Ltd
Waikiki, WA 6169

First published by Serenity Press (Serenity Press Kids) in 2021
www.serenitypress.org

Copyright © Leanne Murner 2021

All rights reserved. No part of this publication may be reproduced, stored in a retrieval system, or transmitted in any form or by any means, electronic, mechanical, photocopying, recording or otherwise, without the prior written permission of the publisher.

National Library of Australia
Cataloguing in-Publication entry

Murner, Leanne (Leanne, Murner), Luca and the Coastal Wattle

ISBN: 978-0-6452689-1-1 (hc)
ISBN: 978-0-6452183-8-1 (e)

Copyright © Cover and illustrations by Kat Fox

# Luca and the Coastal Wattle

## Leanne Murner

### Illustrated by Kat Fox

"Look at all the pretty flowers on that tree, Luca," said Poppy John.

"Oh, wow," said Luca, "there are so many!"

"Can I pick some for mummy?" said Luca.

"Luca, look at all the birds having a drink from the flowers," said Poppy John.

"Oh, Poppy, look at the wallaby eating the flowers too."

"Yes, Luca, the wallaby also eats the flowers from the wattle, it is not just birds that eat the flowers," said Poppy John.

"When the wattle tree flowers it is sometimes used as a calendar," said Poppy John.

"A calendar?" asks Luca.

"Yes, when this wattle tree flowers that is a sign that it is spring."

"Look at these pods, Luca. The flowers turn into a pod and in the pod are seeds. Aboriginal people ground these seeds into flour to use in their cooking," said Poppy John.

"Luca, look at this, if I grab some leaves in my hands can you pour a little water onto my hands? See all the liquid is starting to turn white, Luca?" said Poppy John.

"Yes, Poppy, what is it?" said Luca.

"This is wattle soap wash, Luca; it can also be used as a disinfectant to kill germs."

"Seriously?" asks Luca. "Oh, wow, this tree is AMAZING, Poppy."

"What else can this tree be used for, Poppy John?"

"This tree has a very dense timber through the centre of the trunk, it is used by Aboriginal people to make tools and they use the root system to make boomerangs," said Poppy John.

"Witchetty grubs live under the bark of this tree and feed on the soft surface wood called sap wood," said Poppy John. "Once they start to chew into the wood the tree will release a sap to help prevent its timber from being eaten by the grub."

"Did you know, Luca, these are also a food source for Aboriginal people too?" asked Poppy John.

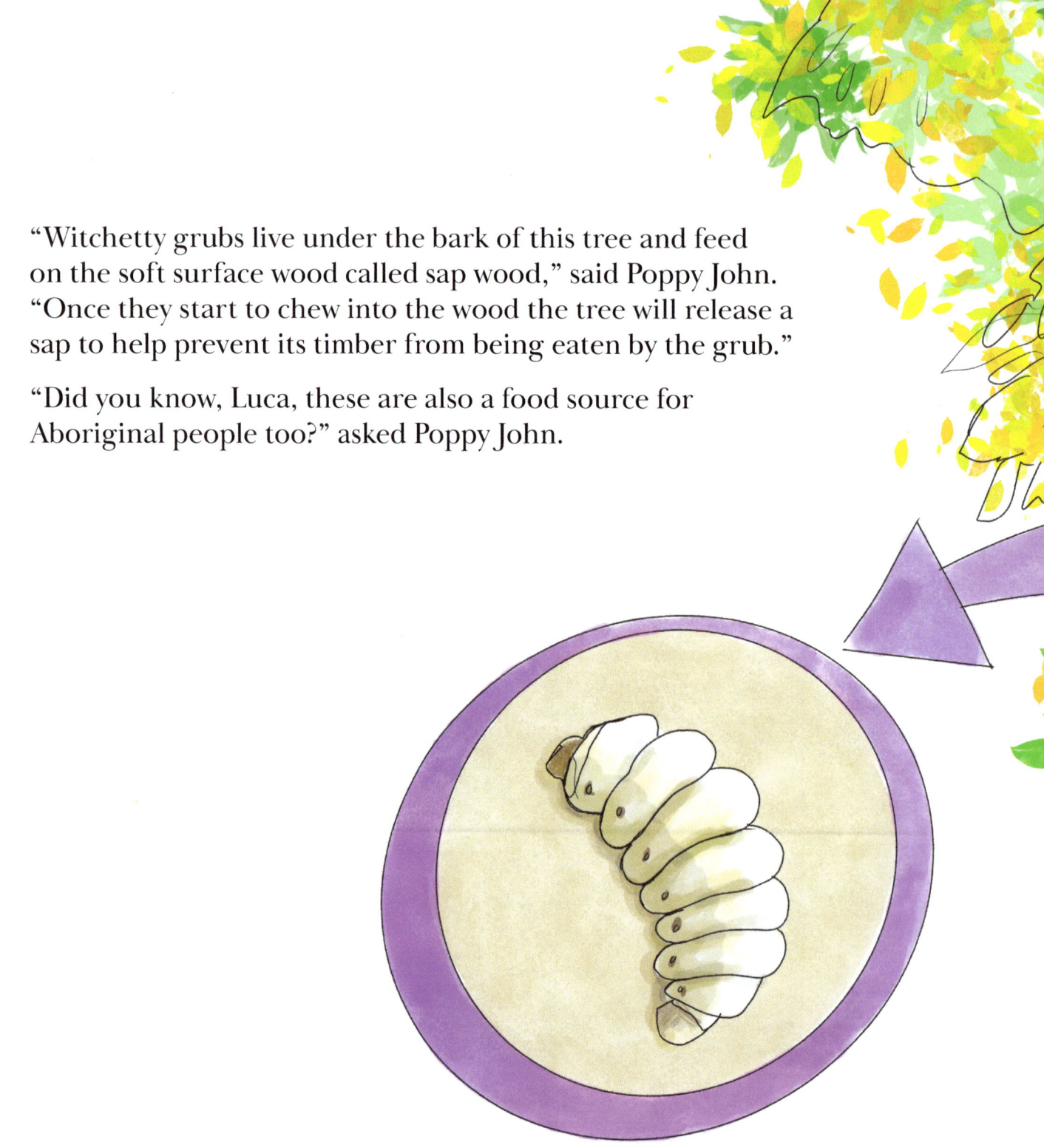

"Luca, these trees are known as nursery crops, they help to feed the soil for others plants to grow," said Poppy John.

"Poppy John, how does it feed the soil?" asked Luca.

"These plants breathe in air and turn it into nitrogen. That then transfers through the roots to the soil to help other plants grow. These plants help shelter seedlings from the sun to help them grow too. Once this tree dies off the plants under it can then grow big," said Poppy John.

"Come on, Luca, let's get these flowers home into some water for mummy," said Poppy John.

"Hey, Poppy, can I take some leaves too, to show my class tomorrow at show and tell?" asked Luca.

"Yes, Luca, that would be a great idea," said Poppy John.

"Look what I picked for you, mummy" said Luca.

"Oh, Luca, they are just so beautiful, thank you," said mummy.

### Galah

The Galah can be easily identified by its rose pink head, neck, and underparts, with a paler pink crown and grey back, wings and undertail. Galahs have a bouncing acrobatic flight but spend much of the day sheltering from heat in the foliage of trees and shrubs. Huge noisy flocks of birds congregate and roost together at night. The flocks feed on seeds, mostly from the ground. Seeds of grasses and cultivated crops are eaten, making these birds agricultural pests in some areas. Birds may travel large distances in search of favourable feeding grounds. The Galah is one of the most abundant and familiar of the Australian parrots, occurring over most of Australia. The nest is a tree hollow or similar location lined with leaves. The female Galah will lay 4 to 6 eggs in her tree hollow but unfortunately only half will usually survive. However, once the chicks make it to adulthood, they will usually live for about 25 years in the wild or up to 80 years when kept as pets. Like other cockatoos, the Galah is an excellent mimic of voices and sounds. Their vocal talents, along with their colour and hilarious personalities, have made them a very popular pet choice.

### Wallaby

Although members of most wallaby species are small, some can grow up to approximately 2 metres in length (from the head to the end of the tail). Their powerful hind legs are used for bounding at high speeds and jumping great heights. Wallabies also have a powerful tail that is used mostly for balance and support. Wallabies are herbivores whose diet consists of a wide range of grasses, vegetables, leaves and other foliage. Wallabies cover vast distances for food and water, which is often scarce in their environment. Mobs of wallabies often congregate around the same water hole during the dry season.

The largest predator of wallabies are dingoes, domestic and feral dogs, feral cats, and red foxes. Wallabies are widely distributed across Australia, particularly in more remote, heavily timbered, or rugged areas.

All wallabies are marsupials: the young, called joeys, are raised in a pouch like a kangaroo.

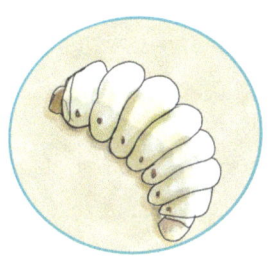

### Witchetty Grub

The Witchetty grub is one of the most famous items on the Aboriginal bush tucker menu. The Witchetty grub is the larval stage (caterpillar) of a large cossid wood moth. The larva eats into the woody roots of the bush and feeds on the root sap. They are the main reason why wattles die within 10 to 15 years. After pupating the wood moth emerges from its woody home as an adult moth, leaving behind its protective skin. The adult Witchetty Moth lacks functional feeding organs. It lives for only a few days on fat reserves, breeding and then dying.

### Wattle

A dense spreading shrub to 3 m tall with flat green oblong leaves. The bright yellow flowers occur along a spike up to 50 mm long. Fruit is a pale brown, curved and twisted pod up to 15 cm long and 8 mm wide, with a beak. Seeds are black, shiny and 4 mm long. The wood, pollen and sap from wattle trees was transformed into food, medicine, weapons, tools, musical instruments, glues, dyes, perfumes, and ceremonial decoration by Aboriginal people. Blooming in spring, the golden flowers also signified seasonal events such as whales arriving on the coast or eels appearing in rivers.

### Rosella

Australia is home to many species of vibrantly coloured rosella, including Crimson Rosellas, Eastern Rosellas, Western Rosellas, Northern Rosellas, Pale-headed Rosellas and Green Rosellas. You will know they are there by their distinctive calls and colourful feathers. These birds are not afraid of people and are a common sight in Australian suburbs and popular visitors to picnics. Rosellas are seen frequently in backyards foraging in the leaf litter for insects or drinking the nectar out of native flowers. Rosellas eat seeds, fruits, nuts, flowers, buds, shoots, nectar, insects and insect larvae. Rosellas are great to have around the backyard, as they will eat bugs and help pollinate the flowers.

# Dedication

I would like to dedicate this book to my best friend and husband. Thank you for supporting me through this amazing journey.

My Luca for being my inspiration, Poppy John for his wealth of knowledge and support.

And to my amazing friend Amy for pushing me out of my comfort zone two years ago, starting my new life purpose.

I would not be here today without you believing in me.

## About the Author

Leanne Murner is an author, business owner/designer at 5 Little Bears Pty Ltd and a proud mum of five boys. Leanne saw a gap in the market for Australian themed wooden toys and began creating products for children with an educational and Australian twist. Being a creative soul Leanne grew the business fast and as time went by her product portfolio increased. In addition she has also published the first two of a series of six children's books, Franki and the Banskia, and Loui and the Grass Tree, with the remaining being published this year. Leanne wanted to teach kids about Australian native flora and fauna, what they are and who needs them to survive. Leanne is busy working on another series of books teaching kids about Australian animals and their habitat, threats and how we can help. Leanne is passionate that our children need to be better educated on Australian wildlife to help keep it from extinction.

www.ingramcontent.com/pod-product-compliance
Lightning Source LLC
Chambersburg PA
CBHW040731150426
42811CB00063B/1576